DATE DUE

FE

JOHNNY TENORIO

by
Carlos Morton

PLAYERS PRESS, Inc.
P.O. Box 1132
Studio City, CA 91614-0132

Johnny Tenorio

© Copyright, 1988, by Carlos Morton
and PLAYERS PRESS, Inc.
ISBN 0-88734-339-2
Library of Congress Catalog Number: 93-19387

Library of Congress Cataloging-in-Publication Data

Morton, Carlos.
    Johnny Tenorio / by Carlos Morton.
        p.   cm.
    ISBN 0-88734-339-2
    1. Don Juan (Legendary character)--Drama.   I. Title.
PS3563.O88194J63   1993
812'.54--dc20
                                        93-19387
                                        CIP

JOHNNY TENORIO

CHARACTERS

JOHNNY TENORIO, twenties, a lady-killer.
BIG BERTA, earthmother, curandera of indeterminate age.
DON JUAN, Johnny's father, fiftysh.
LOUIE MEJÍA, twenties, a would be lady-killer.
ANA MEJÍA, Johnny's novia, Louie's sister. Late teens.

The scene is Big Berta's Bar on the West Side of San Antonio, Texas. At center is a wooden bar with barstools. Atop the bar is an elaborate "altar," the kind used in Mexico during the "Day of the Dead" ceremonies. On one side of the bar, high above the liquor bottles, is a painting of La Virgen de Guadalupe. The bar has the feeling of an arena, with saw dust on the floor—the better to soak up the blood and spittle. Some tables with chairs are interspersed throughout. A gaudy jukebox is in one corner. There is also a front door leading to the outside. Enter BERTA to sing "El Corrido de Juan Charrasqueado."

BERTA: Voy a cantarles un corrido muy mentado. Lo que ha pasado en la hacienda de la flor. (*Enter* JOHNNY *miming the galloping and bucking of a "horse."*)

La triste historia de un ranchero enamorado. (*Echando gritos.*)
Que fue borracho, parrandero y jugador
Juan se llamaba y lo apodaban Charrasqueado,

(JOHNNY *tips his sombrero, reins in, and parks his steed.*)

Era valiente y arriesgado en el amor.
A las mujeres más bonitas se llevaba.
En aquellos campos no quedaba ni una flor.

(*Enter* ANA, *playing the coquette—also wearing calavera mask. Tempo slows.*)

JOHNNY: (*Passionately, he snatches up* ANA *into his arms.*) ¡Véngase conmigo, Mamasota!
ANA: (*Barely protesting.*) !Ay, Señor! ¡Déjeme! ¡Soy Señorita, y estoy prometida!
JOHNNY: ¡Así me gustan más! (*Carrying* ANA *shrieking and kicking offstage.*)
BERTA: Un día domingo que se andaba emborrachando. (*Enter* JOHNNY *with a bottle of tequila.*)

A la cantina le corrieron a avisar
Cuídate, Juan, que por ahí te andan buscando.
Son muchos hombres, no te vayan a matar.

JOHNNY: Pues, que se pongan, ¡a ver quién es el más macho! (*Enter* LOUIE *with calavera mask and gun drawn.*)
BERTA: No tuvo tiempo de montar a su caballo. (*Slow motion:* JOHNNY *mounts his horse as he is shot by* LOUIE.)

5

Pistola en mano se lo echaron de un montón.

JOHNNY: Ando borracho (*Beat.*) y son buen gallo.

BERTA: ¡Cuando una bala atravesó su corazón! (JOHNNY *falls in a heap on the floor as* LOUIE *exits. Two beats.* JOHNNY *sits up abruptly and looks at audience.*)

JOHNNY: ¡Ajúa! (*Letting loose a grito and rising to his feet.*) A mí no me matan tan fácil, ¡cabrones! (*He exits laughing and swaggering.* BERTA *commences to wipe the bar, whistling the corrido as though nothing had happened.*)

DON JUAN: (*Entering bar.*) Berta! Are you open?

BERTA: Claro que sí, pásele, pásele, Don Juan. I was playing one of my favorite rancheritas.

DON JUAN: (*Motioning to the altar.*) ¡Mira no más!

BERTA: You like it?

DON JUAN: ¡Qué emoción!

BERTA: Pues, ya sabe. Hoy es el Día de los Muertos y tonight the souls return to their favorite hangouts. Are you ready?

DON JUAN: Sí, traje mi máscara. (*Showing* BERTA *a calavera mask.*)

BERTA: Wonderful. There will be velorios and speeches expressing el amor and esteem que sentimos por ellos. ¡Esta noche, Don Juan, celebramos a La Muerte! (*Pouring him a tequila.*)

DON JUAN: Pues como dicen los gringos—"I'll drink to that." (*Raising his glass.*)

BERTA: ¡A las almas perdidas! (*They click glasses, drink it in one gulp, and wash it down with slices of lime.*) Ahora, a ver si puedes adivinar—who's altar is that?

DON JUAN: A ver, a ver, a ver. ¡No me digas!

BERTA: Yes, he liked to gamble. (*Holding up the dice.*) And he liked tequila.

DON JUAN: ¡También! (BERTA *shows* DON JUAN *the centerfold of a Playboy magazine.*) He died of this!

DON JUAN: ¡A Chihuahua! ¡Ya sé de quién es!

BERTA: (*Holding up a list.*) Watcha, a list of his conquistas—¿Quieres oírlas?

DON JUAN: No, no, no. (*Visibly shaken.*)

BERTA: You've got to hear this. (BERTA *reads list.*)

In Texas, six hundred and forty.
Arizona, two hundred and thirty.
California, one hundred, and look,
New York, already one thousand!

Among them you'll find
camareras, cantineras
farmer's daughters, city girls
abogadas, tamaleras
there are women of every grade
every form, every stage.

To him all blondes are sexy
Asian women, quite perplexing
English gals are domineering
and Latinas so endearing.

In winter he likes gorditas
in summer, he likes flaquitas
he finds the tall ones challenging
the short ones are always charming.

He'll seduce an older dama
just to add her to his list
and he'll tell the younger girls
"m'hija, you don't know what you've missed!"

He cares not, be they ricas
be they ugly, be they chicas
as long as it's a skirt
he is there to chase and flirt.

DON JUAN: ¡Madre de Dios!

BERTA: Ruega por nosotros.

DON JUAN: (*Crossing himself.*) Y por el alma del difunto.

BERTA: Y sabes que, after every conquest, every amorío, he would
come here a confesarse, to cleanse himself. Big Berta's Bar
was his fuente de la juventud. (*A loud knocking is heard at
the front door.*) Who's there? (*Walking over to the door.*)
We're closed! (*Knocking continues, louder now.*) Pinches
borrachos, cómo friegan. (*Looking through the peephole.*)
¡Es él!

DON JUAN: ¿Quién?

BERTA: ¡El Johnny!

DON JUAN: ¿Juanito?

BERTA: He's early, no lo esperaba hasta medianoche. Ponte tu
máscara, I don't want him to recognize you. (DON JUAN
goes and sits on a bar stool as BERTA *goes to open the door
to let* JOHNNY *in.*)

7

JOHNNY: (*Staggering in, his face a deathly pale.*) Berta! Tequila!
(JOHNNY *sits down slowly, painfully.*)

BERTA: Coming right up. (*She goes behind bar to serve him.*)

JOHNNY: (*To* DON JUAN.) What you doing, playing trick or
treat? (DON JUAN *turns his gaze away and lowers his
head in grief.*) Weird customers you got here, Berta.

BERTA: (*Serving* JOHNNY.) ¿Qué te pasa, Johnny? Your hands
are shaking, you're white as a ghost. And what's this on
your shirt, sangre?

JOHNNY: I got in a fight with a jealous husband. ¡Pinche gringo!

BERTA: ¡Otra vez el burro al trigo! What happened?

JOHNNY: ¿Qué crees? (*Pulls out his gun and lays it on the table.*)
Blam, blam, blam. Laid him low. Bloody scene, wife
screaming hysterically over the body. Police sirens.

BERTA: Ay, Johnny, ¿Por qué te metes siempre en tantos líos?

JOHNNY: (*Patting* BERTA *on the ass.*) I like to live dangerously.

BERTA: (*Slaps his hand hard.*) Johnny, Johnny, let me clean your
wounds.

JOHNNY: No problem, Berta, no problem. Just a minor little
flesh wound. So, where's all the batos locos?

BERTA: (*Picking up his gun and laying it on the altar.*) No te
apures, they'll be around later.

JOHNNY: I haven't been here since ...

BERTA: Since you stabbed Louie Mejía con un filero right here.
(*Pointing to a spot on the floor.*)

JOHNNY: Ay, Berta, you don't have to brag about my exploits.

DON JUAN: ¿Mató a un hombre allí?

JOHNNY: You can almost see the blood stains on the floor.

DON JUAN: Pero, ¿cómo, por qué?

JOHNNY: Because I felt like it.

DON JUAN: ¡Qué lástima!

JOHNNY: Hey, well, it was him or me. Law of the jungle. Snarl,
growl.

DON JUAN: ¡Qué lástima! ¡Que Dios te perdone!

JOHNNY: Hey, look, Pop, I don't need nobody's pardon. Besides,
what's it to you, anyway? (*Walking over to* DON JUAN.)

BERTA: (*Stopping him.*) Never mind, Johnny, he's just a customer.
Toma, otro tequila, on the house. (*She pours him another
tequila.*)

JOHNNY: (*Grabbing* BERTA *by the waist and sitting her on his
lap.*) Hey, Berta, why don't you marry me, huh?

BERTA: Johnny, you're not my type. Además, coqueteas con todas
las rucas—how do I know you'll be true to me?

JOHNNY: Berta, you're my main squeeze. I'd die for you, you know that. (*Trying to kiss her passionately on the lips,* BERTA *disengages. It is a game they always play.*)

BERTA: Johnny, ¿sabes qué día es?

JOHNNY: I don't know, Saturday? It's always Saturday night for me.

BERTA: Johnny, hoy es El Día de los Muertos. Que si te digo que tengo el poder de hacer las almas aparecer. Think I can do it?

JOHNNY: (*Going along with it.*) Of course, you're a curandera.

BERTA: Muy bien, Johnny. Close your eyes, concentrate real hard. (*A flute, high and erie sounds in the distance.*) ¡Escucha! ¿Oyes algo? (*Drum beats.*) These are the sounds of the past, Johnny, sonidos de nuestros antepasados.

JOHNNY: Yeah, I can dig it—Halloween.

BERTA: (*Drums and flutes sound louder. All flashbacks proceeded by this method.*) ¡Qué Halloweenie ni qué mi abuela! I'm talking about Mictla, the underworld, the place where the bones rest. Y aquí llega la primera visita, Johnny, an old friend of yours.

JOHNNY: Louie! (*Enter* LOUIE MEJÍA.)

BERTA: ¿No le reconoces, Johnny? Es Louie Mejía.

JOHNNY: ¡Pinche Louie!

BERTA: ¿Cómo fuiste capaz de matarlo? Why, you were the best of camaradas.

JOHNNY: Yeah, well, cagó el palo. (*Circling* LOUIE. *Drums reach a crescendo.*)

BERTA: You fought because of Ana, ¿verdad?

JOHNNY: Yeah, it all started with that stupid bet to see who would make it with the most rucas in one year. We promised to meet here to compare notes. The winner was to win mil bolas.

LOUIE: (*Embracing and shaking* JOHNNY's *hand.*) Órale, Johnny, mucho tiempo que no te vidrios. ¡Watcha tu tacuche!

JOHNNY: (*Posing, motioning to his suit.*) That's right, from my brim to my taps—reet pleat.

LOUIE: ¡Puro relajo, carajo!

JOHNNY: Pues, ponte abusado, rajado. (*Motioning to* BERTA.) Berta, dos frías.

LOUIE: Same old Johnny. No has cambiado ni un pito. Hombre, this year went by fast, ¿que no? Órale, let's see who is the badest culero in all of San Anto, Tejas. ¿Tienes tus mil bolas?

JOHNNY: (*Laying it down on the table.*) Simón, un grand, dale gas.

LOUIE: Cuando me largué del high school me fui directamente para México.

JOHNNY: When you crossed the Río Grande, did you do the backstroke?

LOUIE: No, hombre, I drove across the bridge en my Low Rider con mi Zoot Suit. The batos went babas, and the huisas went wild. Me fui hasta el D.F.-tú sabes, la mera capirucha.

JOHNNY: What the hell's a "capirucha?"

LOUIE: It means the CAP, the capital. Dig, México is shaped like a huge pirámide, desde la costa hasta la capital. You should check it out.

JOHNNY: Puro pedo. Nunca fui and I ain't going. My folks worked like dogs para largarse.

LOUIE: Well, you don't know what you're missing, ese. Me metí con una de esas niñas popis, las que viven en Lomas de Chapultepec y van de compras en la Zona Rosa.

JOHNNY: You mean, like, she was a Valley Girl?

LOUIE: For sure. Bueno, I turned on some of that Chicano charm and promised to marry her. Su mami nos cachó cochando, ves. Pero la noche antes de la boda me largué con la hermana menor.

BERTA: (*Who has been eavesdropping with* DON JUAN *as the boys guffaw with laughter.*) ¡Qué desgraciado!

LOUIE: I promised to take her with me to Disneylandia pero, nel pastel. ¡Puras papas! La dejé plantada en Monterrey y me largué para San Antonio.

JOHNNY: 'Ta cabrón, Louie. But only two chicks in one year? (*Signals* BERTA *for a couple of tequilas.*) That's not a very good score.

LOUIE: Once I got back to San Anto me clavé 54 más for a grand total of 56!

JOHNNY: How do I know your count is true?

LOUIE: (*Grabbing* BERTA's *hand as she serves them.*) Nomás párate en cualquier esquina del barrio. Count the babes that pass by with my initials tatooed on their hand. (BERTA *slaps his hand, the boys laugh.*)

JOHNNY: ¡Órale pues!

LOUIE: Top that, chingón!

JOHNNY: I took the Greyhound al norte—to the Big Manzana. New York, New York—so big you gotta say it twice. Ended up in Spanish Harlem. One thing I noticed, if I told people I was a Puerto Rican they treated me like dirt.

LOUIE: ¿No quieren a los puertorriqueños allá?

JOHNNY: Nope, the gringos treat them like "Mescins" in Texas.

LOUIE: ¡Qué gacho!

JOHNNY: But if I told the bolillos I was a Chicano, they were really nice to me.

LOUIE: ¿Por qué?

JOHNNY: I don't know, something to do with "good karma."

LOUIE: Karma? What's karma?

JOHNNY: I don't know, something to do with the Indians. I think it has to do with Mexican food or the pyramids.

LOUIE: No hombre, knowing you, les dijiste que eras "Spanish."

JOHNNY: Hey man, you know I would never deny mi Raza. Anyway, we used to make menudo sometimes and invite the gringos over for breakfast. Of course, we knew they wouldn't eat it if we told them it was pancita de res. So we served it as "American Indian Stew!" they scarfed it up!

LOUIE: ¡Qué loco!

JOHNNY: Pinches gringos. Hey, but the white girls—¡mamasotas! They had never laid—and I do mean LAID—eyes on such a handsome Chicano like me. I ate them up. Anglos, Jews, Czechs, Irish, Italians, Swedes ... it was like the United Nations. I took them away from their fathers, boyfriends, husbands. I would even go down to the Port Authority and pick up runaways. (*Flashback. Flutes and drums. Enter* ANA *in blonde wig dressed as a "RUNAWAY."* JOHNNY *walks into the bus station.*) Hey, Mama, what's happening? Where you from, girl?

RUNAWAY: California.

JOHNNY: Califas? So am I! What part?

RUNAWAY: San Diego.

JOHNNY: San Dedo! All right, I'm from San Diego myself. What a coincidence.

RUNAWAY: Really?

JOHNNY: You're my homegirl. Hey, you wanna go party? I got some marihuana. You look like you're hungry. You wanna go get a hamburger?

RUNAWAY: No thanks.

JOHNNY: (*Giving her money.*) Here, have some bread. You can buy something to eat. Go ahead, take it, man, I'll check you later. (*He walks away.*)

RUNAWAY: Wait a minute ...

JOHNNY: This your first time in the city? (*She nods her head "yes."*) What are you doing here?

RUNAWAY: I ran away from home.

JOHNNY: You ran away from home? (JOHNNY *picks up her bag.*) I got a nice pad you can stay at. How old are you, anyways?

RUNAWAY: Eighteen, Well, fourteen, really. (JOHNNY *takes her by the hand. She exits. End of flashback.*)

BERTA: (*To* DON JUAN.) That's what I forgot, marihuana! (BERTA *takes some marihuana cigarettes and places them on the altar.*)

JOHNNY: Then I turned them out on the streets to turn tricks.

LOUIE: You pimped them?

JOHNNY: Yeah. I was actually doing them a favor. I sprang them out of jail if they got busted, had the doc check them out for social diseases. I took care of my ladies, bro. Besides, some other dude would have got them if I didn't.

LOUIE: ¡Qué desmadre! ¿Y cuántas en total?

JOHNNY: Seventy-two. Six I married. You lose. Pay up!

LOUIE: No te lo creo.

JOHNNY: (*Tossing a packet of legal documents on the table.*) Here's the paternity suits and copies of the police records. I should have been a Turk, I had a fucking harem.

LOUIE: ¡Qué bárbaro! ¡Y puras gringas! (*Looking over the documents.*)

JOHNNY: They're the easiest.

LOUIE: ¿Por qué?

JOHNNY: Women's Lib.

LOUIE:

¿Cuántas horas has de emplear
Para cada ruca que vas a amar?

JOHNNY: One hour to fall in love with them. Another to make it with them. A third to abandon them and sixty seconds to forget them.

LOUIE: ¡Chingao! No puedo compararme contigo. (*Giving* JOHNNY *his money.*)

JOHNNY: Why try? There's only one Johnny Tenorio! (*Scooping up the money.*)

12

LOUIE: Alguien te lo va a cobrar un día.

JOHNNY: Tan largo me lo fías. (BERTA, DON JUAN *and* LOUIE *do a double take on that line.*) But say, would you like a chance to win your money back?

LOUIE: ¡Simón que yes!

JOHNNY: You have a sister.

LOUIE: Ana?

JOHNNY: She's fine.

LOUIE: Estás loco, apenas tiene quince años.

JOHNNY: I told you I like fresh meat.

LOUIE: ¡Ahora sí que me estás cayendo gordo, buey!

JOHNNY: ¿A ver? ¿No crees que la puedo hacer caer?

LOUIE: Ponte abusado, ¡malvado!

JOHNNY: ¡No me chingues, chango!

LOUIE: ¡Puro pedo, puto! (*They go for each other, knocking down chairs, glasses, etc. They both pull out knives at the same time.* JOHNNY *disarms* LOUIE, *knocks him down and is about to stab him when* BERTA *stops him with a wave of her hand.*)

BERTA: ¡Cálmala, Johnny! (LOUIE *freezes.*)

JOHNNY: What?

BERTA: Ya lo mataste una vez. Do you want to kill him again?

JOHNNY: (*Backing off.*) Pues no, not if he's already dead.

BERTA: ¡Qué lástima, Johnny!—you had a lot of good times together.

JOHNNY: Yeah.

BERTA: Era como tu hermano, you married his sister. ¿Por qué lo hiciste? (LOUIE *exits.*)

JOHNNY: No sé, Berta, it was either him or me. La Ley del Barrio. (JOHNNY *exits.*)

DON JUAN: ¡Ya no puede ver más! (*Taking off his mask.*)

BERTA: ¿Cómo que no?

DON JUAN: ¡Qué triste tragedia!

BERTA: Más parece una comedia. Ándale—sit back, have another tequila. (*Going to pour him another shot.*)

DON JUAN: (*Stopping her hand.*) ¡No quiero más!

BERTA: At least you know when to stop—él no.

DON JUAN: Do you think that the sins of the father are visited upon the son?

BERTA: Don Juan, con todo respeto, I am not here to accuse anyone. I am merely telling Johnny's story, an old cuento todos conocen. Algunos dicen que empezó en España,

13

others say it is a legacy of the Moors. All I know is él vive—in all of us.

DON JUAN: Síguele pues. (*Putting his mask back on.*)

BERTA: Ahora llamaré al espíritu de Ana. (*Flutes and drums. Enter* ANA *in a Catholic schoolgirl uniform, carrying her schoolbooks.*) Ana, as she once was. Johnny! Johnny! Tell us what happened to Ana. Don't tell me you didn't love her. Yo te conozco, mosco.

JOHNNY: (*Re-entering.*) Love? I don't know what the word means, Berta.

BERTA: Why didn't you try to learn more about el verdadero amor, Johnny, rather than playing at it.

JOHNNY: I'm a player, Berta.

BERTA: Then, play this scene out. (BERTA *snaps her fingers.*)

JOHNNY: (*Crossing to* ANA.) Hi, Ana!

ANA: Hello Johnny. Are you looking for Louie?

JOHNNY: No, I was looking for you.

ANA: Me?

JOHNNY: Can I give you a ride somewhere?

ANA: No thanks, I have to get to school.

JOHNNY: I've been wanting to talk to you.

ANA: Really? About what?

JOHNNY: Things weighing heavy on my mind. (ANA *stops,* JOHNNY *touches her shoulder.*) Your skin is so soft and fine.

ANA: Excuse me, but I'm late for class.

JOHNNY: Do you want to go cruising after school?

ANA: I don't know. I have a lot of homework. I really have to go now. Bye! (ANA *turns away from* JOHNNY, *freezes.*)

BERTA: So, you weren't very successful at first, eh?

JOHNNY: No. But I never gave up. I waited for her every day after school. You see, that's how you break down their resistance.

BERTA: Hmmmm. Cuéntame.

JOHNNY: Well, one day we had a coke at the Cinco y Diez. (ANA *unfreezes as they both sit down at a table.*) So, there, you see? I'm not going to bite.

ANA: You have such a reputation as a lady-killer. They say you're after one thing and one thing only.

JOHNNY: Sure, I can get plenty of girls. Every day, every hour, every minute if I want to. But there's more to it than that.

ANA: What do you look for in a girl?

JOHNNY: Someone I can talk to. Sometimes I wish I had a sister just like you.

ANA: Don't you have any women friends? You know, just friends.

JOHNNY: Sure, one of my best friends is Berta, the bartender at Big Berta's Bar on Guadalupe Street.

ANA: What's she like?

JOHNNY: She's someone I can tell my troubles to. She listens to me and makes the pain go away.

ANA: I'll listen to you, Johnny.

JOHNNY: (*Rising up to leave.*) Well, listen, it is kind of crowded here. Wouldn't you rather go to my place? (ANA *freezes.*)

BERTA: (*Butting in.*) Just a minute here. You really think you know a lot about us mujeres, don't you?

JOHNNY: Yeah, well, that's what I studied in school, Berta.

BERTA: What school? You dropped out.

JOHNNY: The School of Love, baby. That's how come I knew Ana was grade "A." It took me three months of lecturing before she took her final exam. Sabes qué, Berta, maybe it's true what they say about us Latin Lovers.

BERTA: Johnny, esa cosa de los Latin Lovers es un myth.

JOHNNY: Exactly!

BERTA: Bueno pues, entonces—¿qué pasó?

JOHNNY: Hey, the serpent got Eva to eat the apple, ¿que no? (*Crossing to* ANA)

ANA: So, this is your famous apartment.

JOHNNY: What, you don't like it?

ANA: No, it's just I've heard so much about it, I can't believe I'm here.

JOHNNY: Well, from now on you're going to be the only one.

ANA: Ay, Johnny, you're just saying that.

JOHNNY: No, I'm not. See this? (*Matching his palms to hers.*) A gypsy told me how to find the right match. (*Romantic guitar music plays.*)

ANA: Your hand is bigger than mine.

JOHNNY: Ah, but our love lines match!

ANA: Do you believe in all that? Do you really think you'll ever find a woman that'll really satisfy you?

JOHNNY: (*Kissing her.*) I think I just did. (*He holds her close.*)

ANA: Johnny ... don't.

JOHNNY: Why not?

ANA: I want it to be special. (JOHNNY *opens her blouse.*)

15

JOHNNY: You are special to me, Ann, really. (JOHNNY *goes down on his knees.*) I adore you, I worship you! (*Lights begin to fade on them.*)

BERTA: (*To* DON JUAN.) Does this look familiar, Don Juan?

DON JUAN: Desgraciadamente.

BERTA: (*Calling out.*) Bueno, Johnny, dime, did Ana change you?

JOHNNY: She did, Berta, she did. You might say she deflected me from the meteorite course of my destiny.

BERTA: Where did you learn such big words, Johnny?

JOHNNY: I didn't go to college, but I'm not stupid. I even know a little Shaky-es-pear!

BERTA: Bueno pues, sigue el cuento.

ANA: (*Entering, buttoning her blouse.*) Well, its over. You got what you wanted, right?

JOHNNY: I want more than that, Ann.

ANA: Like what?

JOHNNY: Your alma.

ANA: (*Turning to go.*) Adiós.

JOHNNY: Come on, baby, you're not mad at me, are you?

ANA: I guess I'm just mad at myself.

JOHNNY: Where are you going?

ANA: Home. It's late. Mis padres are probably wondering what happened to me.

JOHNNY: Stay here. You don't have to go home. You're a woman now, mi mujer.

ANA: I don't think so, bato. And stop calling me "Ann." Mi nombre es Ana.

JOHNNY: ¡Ana, pues! Ana, you've touched me somewhere I didn't know existed, here en mi corazón. When you're not around me duele.

ANA: Even if it was true, it's just not going to work. I'm only fifteen and you're twenty. Mi hermano will kill you.

JOHNNY: Ana, do you know the story of Romeo and Juliet?

ANA: Of course, I saw the movie.

JOHNNY: Well, Juliet was only fourteen, and she had a relative who hated Romeo. Yet, their amor survived for all time.

ANA: But they both died, cabrón! No thanks! I like you, Johnny, te quiero mucho. But you're nothing but trouble for a girl. I don't know why I went to bed with you in the first place, por pendeja.

JOHNNY: Because you wanted to, Ana. It's our destino. Look, I used to run around with las gringas. They wanted to get down, tú sabes, get married and have kids. But I couldn't. I was searching, sin saberlo, for a Chicana.

ANA: Oh, Johnny.

JOHNNY: Someone of my own Raza ...

ANA: Stop it ...

JOHNNY: Como tú.

ANA: I want to believe you sooooo much.

JOHNNY: Ana, I'd do anything for you.

ANA: Anything?

JOHNNY: Sí.

ANA: Then, wait for me.

JOHNNY: Wait for you?

ANA: If you love me you'll wait until I finish high school. You'll wait for me like a real amigo.

JOHNNY: ¡Amigo! You mean you don't want to fuck me!

ANA: See! I knew it! That's the only thing you want. ¡Te odio!

JOHNNY: Bueno, bueno. We'll do it your way.

ANA: No te lo creo, not one word!

JOHNNY: (*Embracing her.*) I'll prove it to you, mi amor. Just give me a chance. Lo haré por ti. (*Kissing her.*)

ANA: ¿De veras, Johnny? You promise? (JOHNNY *nods his head "yes." A long passionate kiss.* ANA *backs away into another "space."*)

BERTA: How long did you remain "friends," Johnny?

JOHNNY: Long enough, long enough.

ANA: (*On another part of the stage,* ANA *has run into* LOUIE.) You're not going to tell me who to see and who not to see.

LOUIE: Anybody but him, Ana, él es veneno.

ANA: Es mi amigo, my best friend.

LOUIE: ¡Es un hijo de la chingada!

ANA: Don't talk that way about him.

LOUIE: Sólo estoy tratando de cuidarte. I know him very well.

ANA: Like you know yourself, Mr. Hipócrita? The word was out on you, big brother—find 'em, fuck 'em and forget 'em.

LOUIE: Okay. Eso era antes. You know I'm getting married to Inés. Sure, I used to do that stuff, but you have to grow up sometime. Johnny nunca va a ser hombre.

ANA: If you can do it, why not Johnny? Louie, we're all very proud of you, going to night school, working days. And now you're getting married to a wonderful girl. But you have to let me live my own life. I'm sixteen years old now, no soy una esquincle.

LOUIE: But you don't understand this guy—créelo cuando te digo, he's a worm, a víbora, a vampire. He'll suck your blood and leave you dry! Si lo veo contigo, lo mato, I'll kill him! (*Exit* LOUIE.)

ANA: (*Going over to* JOHNNY *and hugging him.*) I don't care what anybody says about you; te quiero, I love you with all my corazón.

JOHNNY: I won't disappoint you, Ana. What you've told me has changed my way of thinking. I'm going to talk to your padres and ask for your hand in marriage.

ANA: Yeah, but I have to finish school, find a career.

JOHNNY: Don't worry, I'll put you through college! And I'm going to clean up my act, no more hustling or selling drugs. I'm going to get a regular job.

ANA: Johnny, I know you can do it.

JOHNNY: Yeah, it's time I stopped acting like a punk kid and started acting como un hombre.

ANA: (*Pulling out a cross and chain.*) Johnny, here, it's a cross the monjas gave me for my First Holy Communion.

JOHNNY: No, I couldn't, really.

ANA: Please, I want you to have it. When you're in trouble think about me. It will give you strength.

JOHNNY: (*Taking the cross, reluctantly.*) Yes, I'm going to need lots of prayers.

ANA: What do you mean?

JOHNNY: Well, before I start my new life, you see, I'm going to have to pay off all my debts. I owe some very important gente a lot of lana.

ANA: Well, they're just going to have to wait.

JOHNNY: You don't understand, Ana. These people don't wait for anybody. They want their money now, or they break your legs.

ANA: Don't worry, Johnny, we'll find a way. Mi cruz nunca falla, my cross never fails. (ANA *exits.* JOHNNY *walks towards the bar, sadly fingering the cross.*)

BERTA: That was two years ago. ¿Nunca terminó Ana la high school?

JOHNNY: No, she had to go out and get a job.

BERTA: ¿Y qué de la universidad y su career?

JOHNNY: Why are you asking me these questions, Berta?

BERTA: La dejaste embarazada, didn't you?

JOHNNY: Pregnant—yes! That's what she wanted!

BERTA: Off course, nunca te casaste con ella. (BERTA *takes the cross away from* JOHNNY *and places it reverently on the altar.*)

JOHNNY: No, but we were living together, isn't that the same damn thing!

DON JUAN: (*Suddenly exploding in a fit of anger.*) No puedo escucharte, vil Johnny, porque recelo que hay algún rayo en el cielo preparado a aniquilarte.

JOHNNY: What's that you say, viejo?

DON JUAN: Ah! No pudiendo creer lo que de ti me decían, confiando en que mentían, vine esta noche a verte. Sigue, pues, con ciego afán en tu torpe frenesí; más nunca vuelvas a mí. No te conozco, Johnny.

JOHNNY: (*Advancing towards him.*) What the hell do I care what you think.

DON JUAN: Adiós, pues. Mas, no te olvides de que hay un Dios justiciero.

JOHNNY: (*Grabbing* DON JUAN.) Just a Goddamn minute!

DON JUAN: ¿Qué quieres?

JOHNNY: Who are you? Take off that mask.

DON JUAN: (*Pushing him off.*) No, en vano me lo pides.

JOHNNY: (*Unmasking him.*) Show me your face!

DON JUAN: ¡Villano!

JOHNNY: ¡Papá!

BERTA: That's right, Johnny, es tu padre. You haven't seen him in años, ever since you left home to raise hell. (*Flutes and drums. Slow motion flashback.* JOHNNY *reverts to age seven.* DON JUAN *becomes a much younger man.*) What was it like when you were chico, Johnny? ¿No lo quisiste?

JOHNNY: Papá, no quiero ir a la escuela.

DON JUAN: Pero hijo, tienes que ir.

JOHNNY: Papá, todos los bolillos hacen fun de mí.

DON JUAN: Cómo que hacen "fun" de ti?

JOHNNY: Durante el lonche, todos ellos comen sanwiches. Cuando saco mis tacos, se empiezan a reír.

DON JUAN: No les hagas caso.

JOHNNY: Y un día mi paper bag estaba greasy y me llamaron "greaser."

DON JUAN: Okay. Empezando mañana puedes llevar sanwiches.

JOHNNY: Okay. ¡Qué suave! (*Thinking about it.*) Sabes qué, mejor no. No me gustan los sanwiches de frijol ... ni de chorizo.

DON JUAN: Bueno, ya apúrate, que se está haciendo tarde.

JOHNNY: No quiero ir, Papá, hacen fun de mí—especialmente la "tee-cher."

DON JUAN: La "tee-shirt?" ¿La camiseta?

JOHNNY: No, la tee-shirt no, la "tee-cher," Mrs. Blaha.

DON JUAN: (*Laughing.*) ¡Oh, la maestra, la Señora Blaha! ¿Qué dice ella?

JOHNNY: After playground me dijo, "Johnny, washe you hans porque dey durty." Me las lavé y entonces me hizo show them en front of everybody.

DON JUAN: ¿Y qué?

JOHNNY: Entonces dijo, "Well, Johnny, you hans so braun I can tell if they clean o no!"

DON JUAN: Ahora sí que no ...

JOHNNY: Y un día la tee-cher me llamó un bad nombre—me llamó "spic."

DON JUAN: ¡No me digas! ¡Conque te llamó "spic!"

JOHNNY: Sí, dijo, "Johnny, you no no how to spick good English!"

DON JUAN: ¡Ay, mi hijo! Por eso tienes que ir a la escuela. Tu mamacita y yo, que en paz descanse, no pudimos ir. ¿No ves como tienes problemas con el Inglich?

JOHNNY: A mí no me importa. ¡No quiero hablar el English!

DON JUAN: ¡No, eso no! ¡Me lo vas a aprender a huevo! Mira nomás. Estoy trabajando como un burro para que puedas educarte.

JOHNNY: I don't care. Trabajo como un burro yo también!

DON JUAN: No, señor. Un hijo mío nunca se raja.

JOHNNY: Pero el Gregy Weiner me quiere beat up. Mira, he hit me right here. (*Enter* LOUIE *in a blonde wig, dressed as* "GREGY.") Can I play with you?

GREGY: No, you can't even speak English, beaner.

JOHNNY: Don't you call me dat!

GREGY: What are you going to do about it, beaner! Brown like a bean! Chili dipper!

JOHNNY: No, I'm not!

GREGY: Yes, you are! (*Hitting* JOHNNY.)

DON JUAN: (*As* JOHNNY *cries.*) ¡Te pegó y no se lo regresaste! ¡Ve y dale en la madre!

JOHNNY: Pero, he's bigger than me!

DON JUAN: Ya te dije, un hijo mío no se raja. ¡Pégale! Si no, yo te pego a ti.

GREGY: Spic! Greaser! Wetback!

JOHNNY: (*Rushing in, flailing with his fists, he gets a lucky shot on* GREGY.) Gringo! Gabacho! Redneck!

GREGY: Teacher! Teacher! (*Running off.*)

DON JUAN: ¡Ahora sí eres hombre! ¿Por qué lloras? Solo las mujeres y los jotos lloran. Ni modo, Johnny, tuviste que aprender a huevo. Ahora, dime, ¿qué dijiste que querías ser cuando seas grande?

JOHNNY: Un astronaut, Papá.

DON JUAN: Ya ves, el primer astronauta chicano. Por eso tienes que ir a la escuela. Vas a ser el primer astronauta que come tacos en el espacio.

JOHNNY: Wow! Tacos in outer space!

DON JUAN: ¡Y mira lo que tengo para mi astronauta! (*Giving* JOHNNY *a new lunch pail.*)

JOHNNY: Oh boy, Papá, un Star Wars lunch pail! (DON JUAN *starts walking away from* JOHNNY. *End of flashback.*) ¿Papá? ¡Papá! Pa ... pá.

DON JUAN: (*As the older man.*) ¡Mientes, no lo fui jamás!

JOHNNY: Then ... go to hell!

DON JUAN: ¡Hijos como tú son hijos de Satanás!

JOHNNY: Fuck you!

DON JUAN: Johnny, en brazos del vicio desolado te abandono. Me matas, mas te perdono. Que Dios es el Santo Juicio. (DON JUAN *exits.*)

BERTA: (JOHNNY *drops down on his knees and bows his head, clutching his lunchpail.* BERTA *goes and tries to console him.*) Triqui tran, triqui tran; los maderos de San Juan. (*Singing a haunting melody as she runs her fingers through his hair.*) Piden pan, no les dan; piden queso, les dan un hueso que se les atoran en el pescuezo. (*Beat.*) Did you love your papá, Johnny?

JOHNNY: Yeah, I guess so. But, that's life in the big city.

BERTA: Do you know that you and your father are very much alike? (BERTA *takes the lunch pail and places it reverently on the altar.*)

JOHNNY: What are you doing?

BERTA: Nada, Johnny, just picking up the pieces.

JOHNNY: You're playing some kind of weird game here, aren't you, Berta?

BERTA: No es un juego, it's for real.

JOHNNY: Why did you bring my father into this?

BERTA: Tu padre te crió—he raised you after your mother died, ¿verdad?

JOHNNY: I didn't need him, I didn't need nobody.

BERTA: Nunca lo conociste, just like you never knew your mother.

JOHNNY: You know my mother died when I was born.

BERTA: Era una mujer muy hermosa.

JOHNNY: That's probably where I get my good looks.

BERTA: Sabes qué, she looked a lot like Ana. (*Flutes and drums, enter* ANA, *pregnant, as* JOHNNY's MOTHER.)

JOHNNY: Mamá ...

BERTA: She was pregnant with you. Tu papá había recién llegado de la Ciudad de México con su sobrina, María. (*Enter* DON JUAN *as a young man.*)

MOTHER: Is your niece all settled in the spare bedroom?

DON JUAN: Sí, no te preocupes por ella. En México vivía amontonada en un cuarto con tres hermanas.

MOTHER: She's a very pretty girl.

DON JUAN: Sí, alguien se la va a robar uno de estos días. ¿Cómo te sientes, querida?

MOTHER: I think the baby is going to be a varón—he kicks like a little bull.

DON JUAN: Un torito. Lo nombraremos Juan, como yo, como mi padre.

MOTHER: Johnny!

DON JUAN: ¡Juan, mi hijo no va a ser gringo! Ojalá que salga como mi padre, alto y güero con ojos verdes. Todas las mujeres estaban locas por él.

MOTHER: Wasn't your mother jealous?

DON JUAN: ¿Qué podía decir? Los hombres—hombres, el trigo—trigo.

MOTHER: ¡Ay sí!

DON JUAN: Tuvo tres mujeres, aparte de mi madre. ¡Tengo hermanos por dondequiera!

MOTHER: How horrible!

DON JUAN: Pero nunca se casó con otra. Oh no, mi madre era su único amor.

MOTHER: I don't want to name our son after a mujeriego.

DON JUAN: Mujer, mis padres duraron casados cincuenta años.

MOTHER: Juan, that doesn't mean tu madre didn't suffer.

DON JUAN: Mamá adoraba a mi padre, tanto como él la adoraba.

MOTHER: What if it's a niña, what will we name her then?

DON JUAN: ¡Juana!

MOTHER: Nooo. Let's name her after a flower, como Rosa, Iris o Azalea.

DON JUAN: No, no, no. Las flores se recogen facilitas. Mejor Rosario, Guadalupe, Concepción. O María, como mi sobrina.

MOTHER: Why?

DON JUAN: Porque una hembra deber ser santa o ángel.

MOTHER: ¡Ay, sí! (*Beat.*) As if your niece was so saintly!

DON JUAN: ¿Por qué dices eso, mujer?

MOTHER: Men shouldn't expect us to act the Virgen María while they go out and do what they please.

DON JUAN: Esas ideas te las metieron los gringos. Eso es lo que no me gusta de este país.

MOTHER: What, that we're more liberated than in the old country? Mira, Juan, what would you do if you caught your daughter sleeping around?

DON JUAN: Como dicen los pochos, I'll break her neck!

MOTHER: See how you men are!

DJ & JOHNNY: (*At the same time.* DON JUAN *to the* MOTHER, JOHNNY *to* BERTA.) Why are you telling me this?

BERTA: Para que aprendas, Johnny. (*With a wave of her hands,* BERTA *changes the tone of the scene.*) Look what happened a few days later ...

MOTHER: (*Angry now.*) What were you doing in María's room?

DON JUAN: Nada, querida, nomás quería saber si estaba bien.

MOTHER: (*Seemingly directing her comments to* JOHNNY.) ¡Mentiroso! Now I know where you go at night!

JOHNNY: (*Responding to* MOTHER.) No, no ...

DON JUAN: ¡Te lo juro por Diosito Santo!

MOTHER: (*Back and forth, to both men.*) Tu sobrina, your own niece! How could you!

DON JUAN: No es mi sobrina.

JOHNNY: Then what was she?

BERTA: María was your father's amante, his lover.

MOTHER: (*Falling, clutching her stomach.*) ¡Ay, Dios mío!

BERTA: On top of that, he married her in Mexico.

DON JUAN: Mi amor, querida, ¿qué pasa?

JOHNNY: (*To* DON JUAN.) Don't just stand there, get a doctor. (*Exit* DON JUAN. JOHNNY *goes to* MOTHER.) ¡Mamá! ¡Mamacita! Please don't die!

MOTHER: Promise you'll never betray me!

JOHNNY: I swear, I swear! Juro por Dios Santo.

BERTA: (MOTHER *dies.*) She died shortly after giving birth to you.

JOHNNY: ¡Mamá!

BERTA: Of a broken heart.

JOHNNY: ¿Por qué lo hizo? Why did he do it?

BERTA: Your father paid for it, Johnny. Juan cesó de ser Don Juan. That's why he never remarried.

JOHNNY: Why didn't he tell me?

BERTA: He didn't want you to be like him.

JOHNNY: Oh, my God. I see it all now.

BERTA: What, Johnny?

JOHNNY: The curse!

BERTA: ¿La maldición?

JOHNNY: I'm damned for all time!

BERTA: Do I detect repentance in your voice?

JOHNNY: (*Screaming.*) Hell no!

BERTA: ¿No? (BERTA *starts lighting the candles on the altar. Incense burns.*) Quizás entonces tu deseo se hará realidad.

JOHNNY: What wish?

BERTA: Your death wish.

JOHNNY: What are you talking about?

BERTA: Life after death, la inmortalidad. I lit these velas to show you a vision. See how brightly they burn? Smell the copal incense, the kind the ancients used in their sacred rites. Pray, Johnny, ruega a la Virgen de Guadalupe, Nuestra Señora, Tonantzín.

JOHNNY: ¡Mis ojos!

BERTA: Pronto vas a ver. Now we wait for the souls to return. They'll come to say a few final words.

JOHNNY: I don't want to hear it, Berta. No one ever really cared about me, not my father, not Ana, none of them.

BERTA: (*Serving him food and drink.*) Cálmate. Sit. Mira, I fixed your favorite comida—tamales y atole. Eat. Los otros están por llegar.

JOHNNY: All right. That's more like it. Be sure to invite Louie. Except that he has so many holes in his stomach, I doubt that the food will stay in.

BERTA: No debes burlarte de los muertos, Johnny.

JOHNNY: Hey, Louie! I'm calling you out, man! Berta made some ricos tamales and hot atole. Better hurry before I eat it all up! (LOUIE, *wearing a calavera mask, enters.*)

BERTA: (*Noticing* LOUIE.) Ah, Louie, there you are. Te traigo un plato. You boys have such big appetites, hay que calentar más tamales. (BERTA *exits.*)

JOHNNY: (*Still absorbed in his food.*) Yeah, Louie, sit down and
     ... (*Suddenly noticing him.*) Oh! Another appearance,
     eh? What's with the costume, still playing trick or treat?

LOUIE: ¡Te dije que no te acercaras a Ana!

JOHNNY: (*Pulling out a gun.*) Chíngate, cabrón, nobody tells
     me what to do! (LOUIE *lunges for* JOHNNY, *who shoots*
     LOUIE *in the head.*) I told you not to mess with me!
     (LOUIE *does not fall—he keeps advancing.*) Jesus Christ!

LOUIE: Remember, I'm already dead! ¿Qué te pasa, Johnny?
     ¿Tienes miedo? ¡Tú, el mero chingón! (*Grabbing*
     JOHNNY *by the throat.*)

JOHNNY: ¡Ayyyyyyy! ¡Déjame! Let me go!

LOUIE: (*Dragging* JOHNNY *over to the table.*) No me digas que
     sientes la presencia de la Muerte!

JOHNNY: Get away from me!

LOUIE: (*Grabbing* JOHNNY *by his hair.*) Come! Come! Que ésta
     va a ser tu última cena. (*Pushing his face into the plate,*
     forcing him to eat.)

JOHNNY: What is this horrible stuff?

LOUIE: Tamales de ceniza. (*Forcing him to drink.*)

JOHNNY: Ashes!

LOUIE: ¡Atole de fuego!

JOHNNY: Fire! Why do you make me eat this?

LOUIE: Te doy lo que tú serás.

JOHNNY: Fire and ashes!

LOUIE: ¡Morderás el polvo!

JOHNNY: No!

BERTA: Ya se va terminando tu existencia y es tiempo de pronun-
     ciar tu sentencia.

JOHNNY: My time is not up!

LOUIE: Faltan cinco para las doce. A la media noche no se te
     conoce. Y aquí que vienen conmigo, los que tu eterno
     castigo de Dios reclamando están. (*Enter* ANA *and* DON
     JUAN, *also calaveras. They block* JOHNNY's *escape.*)

JOHNNY: Ann!

ANA: Yes, it's me.

JOHNNY: ¡Papá!

DON JUAN: Si, mi hijo.

JOHNNY: (*Tries to jump behind the bar. Enter* BERTA *dressed as*
     La Catrina *with skull mask.*) Berta!

BERTA: No hay escape, Johnny. You must face them.

JOHNNY: You too!

BERTA: No estoy aquí para juzgarte, Johnny—they are.

DON JUAN: Un punto de contrición da a un alma la salvación y ese punto aún te lo dan.

LOUIE: ¡Imposible! ¿En un momento borrar veinte años malditos de crímenes y delitos?

JOHNNY: Berta! Will I really be saved if I repent?

BERTA: Yes, but only if one of your victims forgives you on this the Day of the Dead.

JOHNNY: (*In a heavily accented Spanish.*) Entonces, perdónenme ustedes, yo no quiero morir. Deseo pedirles disculpas a todos los que hice sufrir.

LOUIE: Empezaremos conmigo, que soy el más ofendido. ¿Por qué me acuchillaste? ¿Por qué te me echaste encima?

JOHNNY: There's no excuse. But it was a fair fight among men. You wanted to be like me, Louie, but you lost, and that's the price you had to pay.

LOUIE: ¿Ven? No tiene excusa. Que le aparezca la lechuza. Si de mi piel hizo carnicera, ¡él también será calavera! (*The feeling of this last scene is that of a bullfight. JOHNNY is the bull and the others are wielding the cape, pike and banderillas.*)

BERTA: ¿Quién sigue?

ANA: (*She is dressed like a whore.*) I am next.

JOHNNY: Ana. You don't want to see me dead, think of our children.

ANA: I am thinking of them. I would rather they not know you, for fear they will become like you.

JOHNNY: No, no, no! I swear to God—I'll change!

BERTA: You repent?

JOHNNY: Sí, I promise to go home and be a good padre y esposo.

ANA: ¡Mentiras! I've heard all this before. He'll go back to chasing women and drinking first change he gets.

JOHNNY: Ana, don't you see I have to change, my life depends on it.

ANA: No, Johnny, you're addicted to your vicios. You contaminate everyone. Look, I gave you all my love and you turned me out to turn tricks!

JOHNNY: But the Mafiosos were going to kill me. You agreed to do it. I didn't force you!

ANA: You manipulated me, Johnny, like you did all the others.

JOHNNY: But Ana, don't you see, it's a curse that's been passed down from generation to generation. I'm a victim, you're a victim, ¡todos somos víctimas!

ANA: That's right, blame everybody but yourself!

JOHNNY: Ana, honey, think about it. You tried to control me, you wanted to channel my energy.

ANA: I wanted a family!

JOHNNY: But I'm not an esposo. I am a hunter!

ANA: (*Laying into him with a vengeance.*) Si mi corazón murió en esa carrera, ¡el mujeriego también será calavera! (*A mournful cry escapes* JOHNNY's *lips.*)

BERTA: ¿Alguien más? Time is almost up.

JOHNNY: ¡Papá! How can you stand there and say nothing after what you did!

DON JUAN: Ya lo sé, y me arrepentiré hasta mis últimos días. Después que murió tu madre, traté de encaminarte hacia una vida mejor. Fracasé. Seguiste la vía chueca.

JOHNNY: Hypocrite!

DON JUAN: Johnny, dile a Dios que te perdone, como Él me perdonó.

JOHNNY: You want me to ask God for a pardon?

DON JUAN: Es lo único que tienes que hacer.

BERTA: Go on, Johnny, ask for forgiveness.

JOHNNY: But I don't believe in God!

DON JUAN: Entonces estás perdido. (JOHNNY *sinks to his knees. Bells toll softly in the distance.*)

BERTA: Johnny, Johnny, you don't really understand what's happening, do you?

JOHNNY: Berta, will you forgive me? (*Throwing himself at her feet, groveling, as though wanting to get back into her womb.*)

BERTA: Johnny, tú nunca me has ofendido.

JOHNNY: I trusted you, Berta. I told you everything.

BERTA: That's right, mi'jo. I cleansed you by listening and understanding. You see, I am the eater of sins, la que se traga los pecados.

JOHNNY: Oh, Berta, you're the only woman I've ever loved! (*Turning to the other skeletons, who have remained deathly still in a silent tableau.*) You see, somebody loves me! (*To* BERTA.) Does this mean I'm saved? Does this mean I've cheated death?

BERTA: No, Johnny. No te burlaste de la muerte. You are already dead.

JOHNNY: What are you talking about!

BERTA: The gringo who caught you in bed with his wife ...

JOHNNY: I killed him!

27

BERTA: Yes, but he mortally wounded you. Has estado muerto por mucho tiempo.

JOHNNY: But ... how?

BERTA: Tu espíritu, tan violento, no descansaba. Y como este es el Día de los Muertos, the night the souls come back to visit, you returned to your old haunts.

JOHNNY: But, touch me, feel me, I'm alive!

BERTA: Vives solamente en nuestras memorias, Johnny. Te estamos recordando in a celebration ... of death.

JOHNNY: (*Beginning to realize.*) Ohhh noooo!

BERTA: Escucha. ¿Oyes las campanas, Johnny? (*Bells toll.*) Do you hear the women praying rosarios? (*Women praying rosaries.*) See the men digging a grave? (*Pointing offstage.*) Es tu tumba, Johnny.

JOHNNY: I've been dead all this time?

BERTA: Así es, Johnny, todos estamos muertos.

JOHNNY: How can that be?

BERTA: Hay más de una manera de morir. You stabbed Louie to death, but you broke Ana's heart.

JOHNNY: What about my father?

BERTA: His faith in you died.

JOHNNY: Y tú, Berta?

BERTA: Ahhhhh, I am not of the dead, but I am neither of the living. You see, I am of the here, then and will be. Ven, Johnny. (*Flutes and drums. Leading him over to the altar which is suddenly brightly lit.*) Look! This is your altar! (BERTA *climbs up a step. In this light it resembles an Aztec pyramid.*) Look! (*Holding up a calavera mask.*) Aquí está tu máscara ... (*Placing death mask on* JOHNNY's *face.*)

JOHNNY: Am I one of you now! Am I one of the living dead!

BERTA: (*A conch shell blows several times.*) Prepare, Johnny prepárate para la inmortalidad!

JOHNNY: I aaaammmmmm deaaaaaddd!! (JOHNNY *screams, his arms raised up to heaven.*)

BERTA: Here is Johnny Tenorio, el Don Juan, a thorn in the soul of la Raza since time immemorial. Ha traicionado a mujeres, asesinado a hombres y causado gran dolor. Por eso decimos ... que muera!

CHORUS: ¡Que muera!

BERTA: But he also stood alone, defied all the rules, and fought the best he knew how. His heart pounds fiercely inside all of us—the men who desire to be like him, the women who lust after him. He is our lover, brother, father and son. Por eso decimos—¡que viva!

CHORUS: ¡Que viva!

JOHNNY: (*After several beats* JOHNNY *jumps down from the altar.*) Pues, entonces, liven up, let's party! (*The other skeletons are scandalized.*) Come on, get the house a round, it's on me! We got all night! (*Grabbing* ANA *and dancing with her.*)

BERTA: Just wait until morning!

The CALAVERAS *grab partners and dance amidst "ajúas" and gritos.*

CORRIDO

Creció la milpa con la lluvia en el potrero
y las palomas van volando al pedregal
bonitos toros llevan hoy al matadero,
que buen caballo va montando el caporal.
Ya las campanas de San Juan están doblando,
todos los fieles se dirigen a rezar,
y por el cerro los rancheros van bajando,
a un hombre muerto que lo llevan a enterrar.
En una choza muy humilde llora un niño,
y las mujeres se aconsejan y se van,
sólo su madre lo consuela con cariño,
mirando al cielo llora y reza por su Juan.
Aquí termino de cantar este corrido
de Juan ranchero, charrasqueado y burlador,
que se creyó de las mujeres consentido,
y fue borracho, parrandero y jugador.

Slow fade as CORRIDO *ends.*

EL FIN

A HANDFUL OF PLAYS

ISBN 0-88734-802-5

An exciting new anthology of plays by Francesco Bi█████. A delightful combination of everyday experiences and well-drawn characters tell some "not-so-everyday" stories.

This collection of one-acts includes:

THE BENCH - *An old woman feeds the birds in the park each day. Content in her loneliness she does not welcome the unsolicited advances of a charming man. His persistance breaks down her protective guard.*

THE PUBLIC BENCH - *A delightful parade of characters take turns using the bench in the park. Part One - Three old women learn about friendship and jealousy. Part Two - A middle aged couple are indirectly involved in a police investigation. Part Three - A young woman is trying to convince her lover to marry her. She knows better than to push him too far or to give him an ultimatum.*

FRANKS AND BEANS - *A woman who feels that her husband doesn't notice her anymore takes desperate steps to get his attention. She pretends to be "writing" a tell-all book about the intimacies of their marriage.*

THE UNEXPECTED RIFT - *Wife suspects that her husband has AIDS. He is undergoing medical tests, has moved in with a male friend, and is not willing to answer her questions or appease her fears.*

WHEN FATE TAKES OVER - *An elderly woman and her male companion are resigned to the fact that her daughters are moving her into a nursing home. Fate, however, takes a humorous and unexpected turn.*

THE SISTERS - *An elderly lady missed a chance, early in her life, for marriage. She is now on the brink of a second chance at marital bliss. She feels her sister is sabotaging this engagement as she had the previous one. In this brief confrontation they both realize that they prefer each other's company instead of male companionship.*

THE WEDDING GOWN - *Stella is upset with her widowed father and his plans to remarry. In an attempt to prevent, what she feels is a disasterous choice of wives, she uses her dead mother's wedding gown to win her point. But, is she right?*

This unique collection offers several acting and directing tour-de-force pieces.

See current catalogue for prices.

CONDITIONED REFLEX

ISBN 0-88734-315-5

A compelling psychological drama by Curtis Zahn. (2m)

A Patient is free-associating with his Analyst during a private session. Contradicting histories come rambling forth as he travels his course of memory, dreams and desires. A forceful experience in theatre offering insight to the psyche of humanity.

ORIGIN OF THE SPECIES

ISBN 0-88734-314-7

A short, comic escapade by Curtis Zahn. (2m , lf)

Harry has difficulty saying "no". Harriett has pursuaded him to spend a quiet afternoon with her. She has brought the wine and is making numerous verbal advances. Shy Harry keeps making excuses to avoid the situation. In the background we see the Burglar going about his business, and listening to, and enjoying, the bizarre antics of this mismatched couple. After meeting with stone-wall resistance, Harriett finally understands Harry's complete disinterest in her sex. Wonderfully brisk dialogue and fast-paced action make this an exceptionally funny outing.

TAPESTRIES

[M.S.]

An intense one-act by Rolland L. Heiss. (3m, 1f)

William McCaffrey has been arrested for bigamy and forgery. He is also suspected of murdering his second wife. This story, told through the eyes of his mother, weaves the many threads of Bill's life to create a complex tapestry...Bill's strong childhood attachment to his grandmother, his non-demonstrative father, his gentle but smothering mother, and finally his jailer. Heiss has succeeded in weaving a tapestry of pain and human frailty.

IF THE SHOE FITS

[M.S.]

A modern, musical retelling of the delightful Old Lady Who Lived In A Shoe, by Victoria S. Peters. (1m, 2f, 8b, 10g)

Mrs. Gander, the lady who lives in a shoe, is a contemporary woman. Her husband has recently abandoned the household leaving her to deal with the mounting bills, taxes, and problems. Loving but hopelessly impractical Mrs. Gander relies heavily on her eldest children to assume the family responsibilities. Can the family that lives together in a shoe pull together and stay together? A magnificently marvelous new musical.

See current catalogue for prices.

PLAYERS PRESS CLASSIC PLAYS
Edited and Introductions by William-Alan Landes

GEORGE BERNARD SHAW COLLECTION

Widowers' Houses
The Philanderer
Mrs. Warren's Profession
Candida
The Devil's Disciple
Arms and the Man
Caesar and Cleopatra
Overruled
* Captain Brassbound's Conversion
You Never Can tell
* Pygmalion
Androcles and the Lion

* Not Yet in Print

ANTON CHEKHOV COLLECTION

The Bear
The Marriage Proposal
The Anniversary
* The Swan Song
The Wedding
* The Cherry Orchard
* Three Sisters
* Ivanov
* The Seagull
* Uncle Vanya
* A Tragedian In Spite of Himself
* On the Harmful Effects of Tobacco

* Not Yet in Print

JAMES M. BARRIE COLLECTION

Pantaloon
The Will
9128   The Twelve Pound Look
Rosalind